# Keegan Discovers

**Written and Illustrated by**
**Kay Saunders**

PublishAmerica
Baltimore

First printing

ISBN: 9781462649259
PUBLISHED BY PUBLISHAMERICA, LLLP
www.publishamerica.com
Baltimore

Printed in the United States of America

This book is dedicated to Cyril my dad and Keegan's "Pampa"

Keegan went to visit Grandpa's house almost every day. Keegan would sit on the floor and play with his toys until one day he began to discover what his grandpa could do.

Home
Sweet
Home

When Keegan was 1, he discovered that Grandpa could read books to him. So every day Keegan would grab his favorite book and he would crawl up into Grandpa's chair, push the newspaper out of the way, and say "Read!" Although Grandpa never said so, he loved these moments sitting with his youngest grandson.

Home Sweet Home
Keegan

When Keegan was 2, he discovered cars and heavy equipment trucks. He also discovered that his Grandpa happened to know a lot about heavy equipment. He knew about dump trucks, excavators, backhoes, and all the others. Now Keegan would crawl up with Grandpa and show him heavy equipment trucks and they would talk about all the important jobs the trucks could do.

Home
Sweet
Home

When Keegan was 3, he discovered that Grandpa loved to work in the yard digging and planting. Keegan liked digging the most, and did his best to do it just as Grandpa said. Grandpa and Keegan would sit side by side digging, planting, and talking.

Grandpa would take Keegan by the hand and they would walk around the yard and look at all the beautiful things they had planted together.

When Keegan was 4, he discovered Grandpa and Grandma went for walks at the park. So Keegan would get on his bike and pedal as fast as he could. Then he would yell "Grandpa look at me!" And Grandpa would look and say "Hey Keegan you're doing great."

When Keegan was 5, he discovered that Grandpa liked to eat pizza and M&Ms just like Keegan did. So together they would sneak M&Ms when Grandma wasn't looking, and for lunch they would eat pizza together.

sshh

When Keegan was 6, he discovered that some of his friends had grandpas too. But none of the other grandpas were like his Grandpa. Keegan discovered that his Grandpa was special in many ways. Keegan loves his Grandpa and Grandpa loves Keegan.

I love You

CPSIA information can be obtained
at www.ICGtesting.com
Printed in the USA
254118LV00001B